GETTING TO KNOW
THE U.S. PRESIDENTS

GEORGE
BUSH

FORTY-FIRST PRESIDENT
1989 – 1993

WRITTEN AND ILLUSTRATED BY MIKE VENEZIA

CHILDREN'S PRESS
AN IMPRINT OF SCHOLASTIC INC.
NEW YORK   TORONTO   LONDON   AUCKLAND   SYDNEY
MEXICO CITY   NEW DELHI   HONG KONG
DANBURY, CONNECTICUT

Reading Consultant: Nanci R. Vargus, Ed.D., Assistant Professor, School of Education, University of Indianapolis

Historical Consultant: Marc J. Selverstone, Ph.D., Assistant Professor, Miller Center of Public Affairs, University of Virginia

Photographs © 2008: AP Images/John Gaps III: 7; Corbis Images: 29 (Jean Louis Atlan/Sygma), 20 (Bettmann), 6 (Bernard Bisson/Sygma), 28 (Maps.com), 11 (Schenectady Museum/Hall of Electrical History Foundation), 22 (Ruaridh Stewart/ZUMA), 32 (Texas A&M University/Reuters); George Bush Presidential Library: 3, 8, 14, 15, 17, 19, 21, 23, 26; Library of Congress/Pat Oliphant: 30.

Colorist for illustrations: Andrew Day

Library of Congress Cataloging-in-Publication Data

Venezia, Mike.
  George Bush / written and illustrated by Mike Venezia.
      p. cm. — (Getting to know the U.S. presidents)
  ISBN-13: 978-0-516-22645-3 (lib. bdg.)   978-0-516-25536-1 (pbk.)
  ISBN-10: 0-516-22645-2 (lib. bdg.)   0-516-25536-3 (pbk.)
  1. Bush, George, 1924—Juvenile literature. 2. Presidents—United
States—Biography—Juvenile literature. I. Title. II. Series.

E882.V46 2008
973.931092—dc22
[B]
                                                        2006102974

President George
Herbert Walker Bush
in the Oval Office of
the White House

George Herbert Walker Bush was the forty-first president of the United States. He was born in Milton, Massachusetts, on June 12, 1924. George H.W. became president in 1989. That was exactly 200 years after the nation's first president, George Washington, was sworn into office.

As president, George Bush was known for his patience and skill in dealing with foreign countries. One of his biggest accomplishments was helping to end the Cold War. This was a war of disagreements, words, and threats, mainly between the United States and the Soviet Union. The Soviet Union was made up of Russia and a group of smaller countries controlled by Russia.

The Cold War started shortly after the end of World War II in 1945. As Russia pushed the Nazi armies back toward Germany, it occupied the smaller European countries that were in its path. It forced those countries to accept the Communist way of life, which was very different from the United States' belief in freedom for all people.

In Poland, people frustrated with Communist rule held labor protests in the late 1980s.

After forty-five years, the citizens of many Eastern European countries began to revolt. They were fed up with the Communist system and with Russia having so much influence over them. They demanded their freedom. President Bush worked with Russian and other world leaders. He wanted to make sure there wouldn't be any violence or hard feelings between the Soviet Union and the rebellious countries they once ruled.

Amazingly, in 1991, the Soviet government kind of just gave up. When its leader, Mikhail Gorbachev, resigned, the Cold War officially ended without even a shot being fired!

The fall of the Berlin Wall in 1989 was a huge symbol that the Cold War was coming to an end. It had been built in 1961 to keep people from leaving Communist-controlled East Berlin, Germany.

George Bush (second from left) and his family

George H.W. Bush grew up in a wealthy family. His parents had a fancy home in Greenwich, Connecticut, and a big summer house near the ocean in Kennebunkport, Maine. Even though George and his three brothers and sister had everything they ever needed, they weren't spoiled.

The Bush kids were brought up never to brag, to be good sports, and to share what they had with others. George was such a generous boy, he got the nickname "Have Half," because he always gave half of what he had to his brothers, sister, or friends.

George H.W. Bush was sent to the best schools. He was a good student, an excellent athlete, and very popular with his classmates. George planned to go to college, but just before he graduated from high school, Japanese warplanes bombed U.S. bases at Pearl Harbor, Hawaii. The United States immediately declared war on Japan and entered World War II. Right then and there, George made up his mind to join the navy air force.

Immediately after the attack on Pearl Harbor (above), George Bush joined the war effort.

As soon as he turned eighteen, George Bush signed up for flight training. One other major event happened at this time, too. George fell in love.

Before he left for his training, George met a girl at a dance. Her name was Barbara Pierce. Right from the start, George and Barbara got along great. They saw as much of each other as possible when George came home on leave. George finished his flight training in 1943,

when he was still eighteen. He learned to fly
a torpedo bomber, and was the youngest pilot
in the U.S. Navy.

George Bush in the cockpit of his torpedo bomber, *Barbara III*

George might have been the youngest pilot in the navy, but he was as brave as anyone. George flew lots of dangerous missions, bombing enemy targets on islands in the Pacific Ocean. He was even shot down twice!

George and Barbara Bush
dancing at their wedding

George always remained calm, though, and managed to escape serious injury both times. While he was still in the navy, George returned home on leave to marry Barbara. When the war ended, he finally got the chance to go to college. George attended Yale University in Connecticut.

When George graduated from Yale, he had to make an important decision. He could either work at his father's investment company in New York City, or take a chance trying the oil-drilling business. George didn't know anything about the oil business, but a friend of the Bush family was willing to teach him.

George started at the bottom position of an oil company in Texas. He had to clean and paint drilling equipment and order machine parts. George learned the business quickly. Soon Barbara and their first son, George W., joined him in the hot, dusty oil fields of Odessa, Texas.

George and Barbara Bush with their first-born son, George W. Bush, in Odessa Texas

George Bush became very successful locating oil. He installed oil drills on land he bought or rented, and soon started up his own company. It wasn't long before George became a millionaire.

During the time his company was growing, George became interested in politics. He had ideas about how to make his state's government work better for business owners and the people who lived in Texas. In 1964, he ran for the U.S. Senate as a Republican, but lost to the Democratic candidate. Then, two years later, he ran for the U.S. House of Representatives. This time he won.

George Bush (left) in the oil fields of Midland, Texas

U.S. Ambassador to the United
Nations George Bush casts a
vote on an issue in 1972.

In Congress,
George was
known to stand
up for the rights
of minorities.
He voted for the
Fair Housing
Act of 1968, an
important law that helped prevent
discrimination. Being a U.S. Representative
led to a whole series of major government jobs
for George H.W. Bush. He was well liked in
Congress, and a number of U.S. presidents liked
him, too. President Richard Nixon appointed
him U.S. ambassador to the United Nations.

Then, in 1974, President Gerald Ford appointed him as a special representative to China. George and Barbara moved to China. They took language lessons there and became popular with the Chinese people and government officials.

George and Barbara Bush riding bikes in Beijing, China, in 1974

In 1975, President Ford asked George Bush to return to Washington, D.C. He wanted Bush to become the director of the Central Intelligence Agency (CIA). George did a great job as CIA director. He told a friend that it was the most interesting job he'd ever had.

In China and as CIA director, George Bush learned a lot of things about dealing with governments of foreign countries. This knowledge would help him later when he became president.

Buttons, badges, and other memorabilia from the 1980 Reagan-Bush presidential campaign

Vice President George Bush and President Ronald Reagan

In 1980, George felt he had enough experience to run for president of the United States. First George had to get the support of the Republican Party in order to be nominated.

Unfortunately for George, he lost to another Republican, Ronald Reagan. Reagan surprised George, though, by asking him to run as his vice president. George was thrilled. In 1980, Ronald Reagan and George Bush won the election.

George served as President Reagan's vice president for two four-year terms. When it was time for the next election, in 1988, George Bush decided to run for president again. Because he was a low-key, nice guy, and not very forceful in his speeches, his opponents tried to make him out to be a weak leader. One national magazine, *Newsweek*, even said George was a wimp!

It seemed an unfair charge for someone who had been a brave war hero. George's campaign team got to work right away to change his image. George agreed he should try to come off as tougher and more decisive.

President and Mrs. Bush wave to the crowd as they walk along the parade route following Bush's inauguration on January 20, 1989.

Voters went along with the tougher, more decisive George Bush, and he won the election. Right away, he had to help solve a major problem.

For years, savings and loans all over the country had been taking their customers' money and investing it foolishly. A savings and loan association is a kind of bank in which the customer's money gets invested in home mortgages. Now these institutions were at risk of going out of business.

President Bush worked with Congress to come up with a plan to bail them out. The plan worked, and the savings accounts of millions of Americans were protected.

A map of the Middle East

Another event President Bush handled successfully was the first Persian Gulf War.

The Gulf War started when Iraqi dictator Saddam Hussein invaded nearby Kuwait. Kuwait is a small Middle Eastern country with a huge oil supply that Saddam wanted. President Bush couldn't stand the idea of an evil dictator invading a peaceful nation. He worked harder than ever, convincing world leaders to form a coalition to fight Iraq.

The well-organized coalition army quickly forced Iraq's troops out of Kuwait. Saddam Hussein and his army were defeated for the time being. President Bush's patience and careful planning got him the highest approval rating of any president in history.

First Lady Barbara Bush and President George Bush celebrated Thanksgiving with U.S. Marines in Saudi Arabia during the Persian Gulf War in 1990.

Even with a high approval rating, George H.W. Bush lost the election when he ran for a second term. People felt the president had done a good job handling world events, but had neglected things at home in the United States. To get elected in the first place, George Bush had promised not to raise taxes. No matter what!

While campaigning for president, George Bush had said, "Read my lips: no new taxes!" This political cartoon by Oliphant criticizes the way he later broke his promise and raised taxes.

After being president for a while, though, he found he had to break his promise. President Bush realized some important government programs needed more money to continue. Breaking such a firm promise disappointed many voters.

Former President Bush (bottom) celebrated his eightieth birthday by going skydiving.

Unfortunately for President Bush, the economy was also in bad shape when the election came up. Prices on almost everything were going up, and many people were out of jobs. President Bush seemed unaware of the situation. In 1992, discouraged voters chose another candidate to be their president. George and Barbara moved back to Texas, where they enjoyed retirement. George Bush spent more time with his grandchildren, kept involved in politics, and even went skydiving for fun.